IMAGES OF
FRANCE

IMAGES OF
FRANCE

Jean-Louis Houdebine

Introduced by
Theodore Zeldin

HAMLYN

Vaux-le-Vicomte Under the soft skies of the Ile-de-France, the parterres and fountains of the gardens laid out by Le Nôtre still adorn the superb château built for Nicolas Fouquet around 1600. At the time he was the Superintendent of Finances, a connoisseur of art and friend of La Fontaine and Molière, as well as of Le Brun, who was responsible for the decoration of the apartments. This noble composition of patterns and forms echoes the rhythmic majesty of heroic verse, and is a perfect example of classical beauty.

First published in 1991 by
Paul Hamlyn Publishing Limited,
part of Reed International Books Limited,
Michelin House, 81 Fulham Road,
London SW3 6RB

ISBN 0-600-57313-3

Produced by Mandarin Offset
Printed and bound in Hong Kong

Introduction

*T*he France that interests me most is the one that is not immediately visible. I like to discover the emotion in the nails and concrete that hold its majestic heritage together. I am not satisfied with driving through villages deciding from the look of a main street whether it is picturesque enough to stop. External appearances are a camouflage. Houses hide behind their regional style, which is what tourists usually come to identify and admire; but I see this style as a warning notice, 'Do not disturb, do not look too hard'. The purpose of conforming to a style is to avoid being noticed. I cannot forget that a big slice of history has been dominated by fear of the evil eye. Most facades say 'I do not wish to be troubled by strangers.' But occasionally they announce without shame, 'Look at me, I can defy my neighbours, people can think what they like, this is the message I wish to proclaim'. Every building, however humble, is a witness of a struggle, of a triumph, of pride of some sort.

So I am not content to use modern guide books to tell me where to go, and not only because they do not bother to mention so many villages on the pretence that there is nothing for the tourist to do. The criteria adopted by guide books are not mine. They believe their readers are interested more in what the eye can see than in smells and sounds, more in inert buildings than in living beings, more in places associated with historical *events than in individuals of the anonymous crowd, and still less in their dreams.*

Straight to the church and the chateau: that is the guide books' order; if there is heavy industry around, they mention it apologetically; but I am interested by industrial estates, even if they are outwardly ugly; France abounds in these sheds and workshops where extraordinary innovations start: there are wonderfully original people to be found there.

Guide books assume that the main interest of a tourist in France, as far as the present day is concerned, is where to eat and sleep. But though these are certainly among the country's justly celebrated delights, I confess that what I want to know even more is where I can have a good conversation. Among the achievements of French civilization the invention of the literary salon ranks highly: there women stopped men being bores talking shop and persuaded them to discuss matters of universal interest in a general way. France is par excellence a country of good talk. French food and wine do not just produce sensual pleasures: they encourage people to talk more nobly. How the cook explains his or her passion for food is often as memorable as the pintadeau au bourgogne et lard fumé; *the warm rhetoric of the innkeeper often compensates for the modesty of a bedroom. No two French people ever seem to say the same thing to me, even if they use the same words. Every greeting has nuances, and every nuance of politeness is food for thought.*

France for me is therefore first of all a country of surprises, a magic garden of the unexpected. Behind every facade, however undistinguished, there is a living soul, which means a mystery. To be content with categorizing individuals or homes into regional classifications is to miss the essential.

Perhaps guide books limit themselves in this way because there is an old myth that it is not easy for a stranger to start a conversation with a French person. It is no longer possible to believe that. The French have become less formal in recent decades, and their curiosity about foreigners, their desire to practise their new foreign language skills, are vastly greater than they used to be. It has been revealed that over half of them would like to invite tourists to lunch or dinner, 61% would like to have an amorous adventure with a foreign tourist, 82% would be happy to act as guides to foreigners visiting their area.

I propose that for the launching of the new Europe in 1992, these desires should be put into practice in a great symbolic gesture: every willing French family should send an invitation card, with blue, white and red borders and the emblem of the republic, inviting a foreign family to lunch. This would do more to reveal the true France than all the banal tourist advertisements which litter magazines and hoardings.

The landscape of France does not just inspire aesthetic sensations in me. When I gaze at it, I see not only what is there, but also the people who are missing from it. The extraordinary feature of its present form is that very few living human beings are to be found in it. Once upon a time, visitors were struck by the very opposite thought. It used to be the most populous country in Europe. When Shakespeare's England contained only five million inhabitants, France already had twenty million. Those interminable fields of the Poitou, for example, planted with kilometres of sunflowers, and visited only by the rare tractor, were once positively inhabited, as the deserted ruins of labourers' cottages remind one. The deserted roads were once trodden by a wonderful variety of artisans carrying their specialized tools on their backs and by Balzacian peasants, carrying in their heads the obsessive desire to buy that precious land. It is now over a century since that passion began to wane, since almost every square metre of France's land ceased to be hungered for and dreamt about and known intimately for its precise, minutely different qualities.

The landscape to be seen today is not entirely the landscape of nature. Humans have done a great deal to change it. Our present determination to protect the beauty of the environment seems to me to be incomplete. I see also the landscape as it was before the industrial and urban developments of the last few centuries: the rural civilization to which we are tempted to look back nostalgically did not always involve peaceful coexistence with nature: it was also a slow war, against the shade and the wildlife of the forests in particular. Trees and hedges have long been the victims of humanity's growing numbers.

Thus the region of the Nord-Pas de Calais appears to be a flat, somewhat dreary landscape, crippled by industrialization, blighted by slag heaps. The Regional Council recently set up a committee to plan a new future for what was once a bee-hive of prosperous activity and is now one of the poorest parts of France. I was invited to be a member.

I proposed that the Nord-Pas de Calais should recreate its landscape anew, instead of contenting itself with protecting its limited beauty spots and with controlling pollution. A landscape reflects the aspirations of its inhabitants as well as the earth's gift. The future of this blighted region, in my view, needs to be not just European but international, if it is not to bleed slowly to death; it has lost half a million young people in our lifetime, because there are more attractive jobs elsewhere. One of the effects of European union may well be that some regions will become deserts and others enormous conurbations of endless suburbia.

I suggested that trees from all over the world which could flourish in the northern climate should be planted, with art, to create new horizons, new undulations, juxtapositions of colour and form which would make a landscape to be found nowhere else. The committee adopted the recommendation. Will it ever be made a reality? It is appropriate that in a democracy there should be an opportunity for the whole community to participate in consciously making an environment. A landscape deserves a plaque commemorating those who have lived in it just as a building does. The inhabitants have nearly always added or taken away something from it, altering the fauna as well as the flora.

It is not only industry that blights a landscape. The Avesnois was only a generation ago a major apple-growing region. It was killed by the Golden Delicious, which was introduced on a mass scale in the south, and sold with more commercial skill. There is now a wonderful living museum of the apple on the outskirts of Lille which preserves 600 varieties, very few of which can be found in the shops. In the old days, apple trees were allowed to grow in meadows, side by side with grazing cows. Now they are segregated. The next fashion in landscapes may well be for more mixtures of different kinds of vegetation.

When I read in a guide book that the forest of Paimpont in Brittany is worth a visit because it is mentioned in the legends of King Arthur, I wish the author would add how the animals, birds and insects in it have changed over the centuries. But of course even less is known of their history than of our own. No one can produce statistics, for example, of the rise and fall of the population of flies in France. Two centuries ago they were tyrannical kings, or at least powerful bandits, in many regions of the south.

The trouble with being shown France by its inhabitants is that they never imagine that they are interesting themselves: they always want to take you to see the local ancient monument or gallery. When I question individuals about themselves, they are surprised that I should find anything worth remembering about their lives, which they assume to be ordinary. Since I cannot speak about them individually here, I shall give three examples of people whom I find particularly worthy of a detour.

Soon the rarest monuments in France will be the peasants. But new forms of communication and employment are making possible a new kind of rural inhabitant, who is not a farmer, but who wants a happier marriage between modern technology and nature. When agriculture becomes an industry, and peasants disappear, a new profession may arise, in the pay of the community, to manage the countryside as a work of art, and ensure that it remains a pleasant place to live in.

The individual who lives in provincial cities is another kind of novelty. The tourist may think that these cities are being restored to their original condition by the cleaning and repair of the central old streets, and by the creation of pedestrian precincts; but something new is in fact being created; an authentic restoration would bring back smells no modern person could tolerate. The novelty lies elsewhere: the provinces no longer lack self confidence. The ablest people, or at least the most ambitious, once escaped to Paris. The new provincial, however, has not used the T.G.V. to make his city into a suburb of Paris. Instead he has made it carry away the old frustration of an inferiority complex. If one lives in Dijon or Tours, it is now possible to enjoy many of the benefits of Paris without its inconveniences. French people are increasingly leading double lives.

Paris is the place where half of the households contain only one person, and two-thirds of these individuals living alone are women. Paris has always been the capital of feminine chic, but now it is more than that. It used to be a city in which there were more men than women, ambitious men; but today the proportions are reversed. Women have in the past imprinted a special character on French culture and behaviour. The most important of all riddles today is: In what direction are women pushing French civilization?

It may appear that all is quiet on this front at the moment. Superficially a return to traditional feminine values is taking place. But I believe this is only a pause for rest and the beginning of reflection. France is no longer a factory for the production of new political ideas. The interest in politics has waned. The road to economic prosperity has been opened. What is of concern now is how individuals should treat each other, how to deal with the emotions. There is a lot of thinking, more or less silent, going on around that theme, and it is women who are doing most of the thinking.

What goes on in people's heads is always uncertain and unpredictable. All that is certain is that by this criterion, France is very much alive and is likely to produce many more surprises in the future.

Theodore Zeldin

The gardens of France When
"cultivating one's garden" becomes
an art . . . This old French tradition
was infused with new life under the
Italian influence of the Renaissance.
It then came into its own with Le
Nôtre and the classicism of the formal
garden, before fashions changed in
favour of the English landscape style.

The Villandry terraces (*opposite*)
with, on three different levels, the
water garden, the decorative garden
whose flowerbeds symbolize the forms
of love, and the vegetable garden
spread out like a well-arranged
primer of vegetables and fruit, are a
perfect example of the Renaissance
garden so typical of the Loire valley.

In Paris, on the edge of the Latin
Quarter, the Luxembourg (*above*)
offers its peaceful, shady walks to
tempt the tired passer-by and to calm
the student in the throes of
examinations, while on its lake
children's boats carry their own
cargoes of hazy dreams.

23 ❈ PATISSERIE ❈ 2

Parfums

vanille
chocolat
café
praliné
pistache
cassis
citron
noix de coco
banane

Pain de Seigle
Raisin
Noix

Pain Complet
Pain de Son
Fougasse
Cramique

Bread and patisserie Bread is the staff of life; bread eaten in secret is sweet; take the bread out of someone's mouth… Every language and country has its sayings about bread. This is particularly true in France and is an indication of the traditional and extremely important part that bread plays in everyday life. And for little treats during the week, and major family occasions at the weekend, there are always those delicious pastries from the patisseries that can be found at the corner of nearly every street.

Every region of France has its own specialities, so much so that you are spoilt for choice. But if you prefer everything to be home-made, well, there is nothing to stop you from making dough or pastry by hand yourself!

French cuisine Few things are quite as picturesque as a market in a southern French town. A brilliant shaft of light strikes a cool stall and falls, beneath the exotic fruit, on a tasteful display of the vast range of produce grown in the South. This array of produce – fennel, artichokes, courgettes, peppers and tomatoes is succulent and vividly coloured. It will be used with red scorpion fish and blue anchovies from the Mediterranean to garnish Niçois salads and Marseillais soups, all redolent of garlic, thyme and basil. Pissaladière and Bouillabaisse, and other regional specialities reflect the warm and colourful personalities of the South and its people.

Meanwhile, in the Ile-de-France, farmers patiently cultivate the heavy, rich earth in their ploughland and fields: wheat becomes crusty bread, and milk creamy cheese. This is how the mild, soft Brie de Meaux cheese, with its white powdery rind, is made by "the dairymen of Brie":

1 Rennet is added to the milk.

2 The curdled milk is placed in wicker trays and left to drain.

3 When the cheese is firm, it is salted all over.

4 After fifteen to twenty days, when it has become covered in white mould, the cheese is taken to the cellar. Here, the soft curd separates into two creamy layers.

5 The cheese is ready to eat when these two layers are nearly touching.

This is the delicate alchemy of cheese, of which there are more than 140 varieties in France.

Pétanque People play pétanque throughout France, but it is under the Provençal sun, in a place like Marseille, near the Old Port, that the game probably assumes its true, momentous nature. Pétanque is all a question of approach. It doesn't matter whether it's ten in the morning, noon, or just before supper, serious business is being conducted beneath the plane trees. It's a clean fight, of course, but that doesn't mean you won't fight to the bitter end. "Come on! Get out of that! . . . Nice one!" (or perhaps "Aah, too bad!"). People shout, moan, and sometimes argue. But make no mistake, this is just for fun; that's why everyone takes it all so seriously. "That confounded jack! . . . Waiter, drinks all round! Same time tomorrow, everyone?"

The Tour de France Every summer since the beginning of the century, France has paid homage to what it calls colloquially "the little queen" – otherwise known as the bicycle. The focus, of course, is a top-level sporting event that attracts the best competitive cyclists from all around the world. But the "Tour" is also a cultural event in which millions of spectators take part. For three long weeks the race snakes along the roads of France and, day after day, everyone has a chance to appreciate the wonderful variety of the French countryside.

Notre-Dame de Paris In the very heart of Paris, at the tip of the "ship" formed by the Ile de la Cité, where the ancient town of Lutetia was founded, looms the cathedral of Notre-Dame. It took more than a century to build (from the end of the 12th century to the 14th century). With the delicate tracery of its façade, its broad nave, the majesty of its four-square towers, the perfect harmony of its two great rose-windows, and the grace of its flying buttresses, it is a dazzling masterpiece of Gothic art. During restoration work in the last century, Violet-le-Duc added a number of large gargoyles around the upper gallery. With their enigmatic gaze these fantastic birds, monsters, devils and chimeras seem to keep unceasing watch over the city and the great river that runs through its centre.

Paris: A city of ceremony and cafés There are few cities in the world that can boast such architectural perspectives as those seen here radiating out from the Place de l'Etoile. This is where all the great commemorative ceremonies and national events are staged, beneath Napoleon's great Arc de Triomphe, the hub of a wheel with twelve broad avenues for spokes. The most famous of these is of course the Champs-Elysées, which leads down to the Place de la Concorde with its obelisk from Luxor, its statues, perched on buildings at its corners, representing the great towns of France, and its two, Roman-inspired, monumental fountains. Centuries of history are represented here: the Tuileries gardens and palace, the Louvre, and in the distance, Notre-Dame. These are the most stylish parts of the capital, a district whose creed, brash or discreet, is that of wealth and elegance. And the justification for calling Paris "the City of Light" is probably nowhere better seen than at night in the Place de la Concorde, or as one walks up the Champs Elysées towards the Place de l'Etoile.

The café, bar and bistro have always been an inseparable part of French life. People go to a café to drink, of course, but mainly to talk. They chat, exchange opinions and jokes, and flirt with one another. It's a place to complain, too, about anything and everything: the Government, the neighbours, the taxman, or the police. People go on their own too, to observe or meditate, to write a letter, a poem or a novel, or maybe just to dream.

Paris: Sacré-Coeur and the Métro It is perhaps every Parisian's dream to live in a apartment overlooking the roofs of Paris with, in the distance, Montmartre and the Sacré-Coeur. Paris wouldn't be Paris without its famous hill, which was once covered in vineyards and windmills. From the end of the last century to the eve of World War II it was the mecca for a cosmopolitan, artistic and somewhat shady community, and its praises were sung by artists and poets. Van Gogh, Picasso, Braque and others all lived and worked here. Although things are probably more lively around Saint-Germain-des-Prés or Les Halles these days, the names of Pigalle and Blanche, and of the Place du Tertre, still conjure up delightful images and memories of night-time strolls through its narrow streets.

From time to time the Métro emerges into the air from its subterranean depths. It does so here at Bir-Hakeim Bridge, where it crosses the Seine over the Ile des Cygnes. The architect responsible for building these stretches of overhead line did so with a deliberate formality that celebrated the staunch Republican virtues of Progress; hence the bronze statues representing, on the downstream side, Electricity and Trade, and upstream, Science and Work.

Paris: Palais de Chaillot The French affinity for monumental architecture has profoundly influenced the Parisian landscape and gives its open spaces a distinctive feel. The Eiffel Tower and the Palais de Chaillot confront one another across the Seine (*left*). The great gilded statues of the Palais overlook the vast expanse of the Trocadéro esplanade.

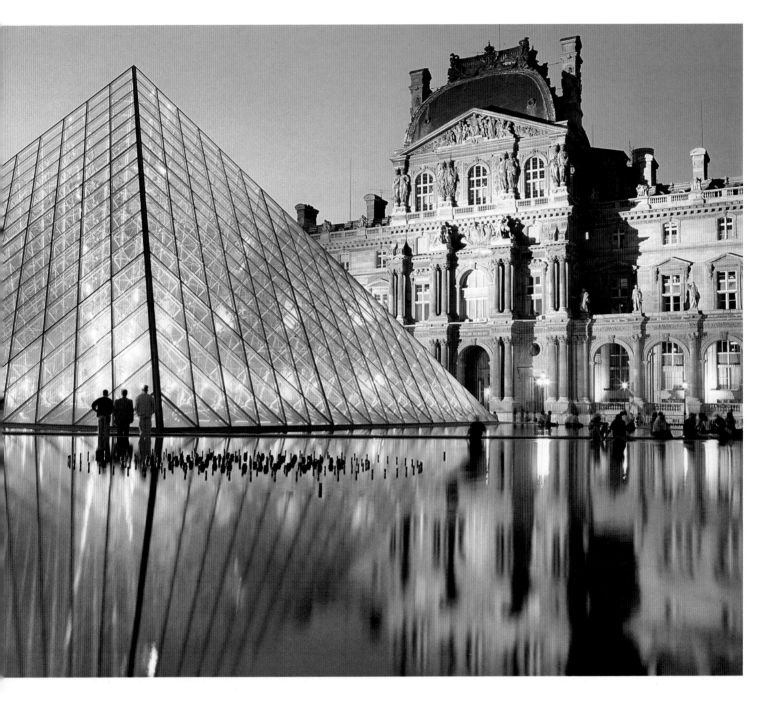

The Louvre pyramid In the Cour Napoléon of the Louvre (*above*), once the palace of the kings of France, but now one of the world's most richly-stocked museums, the giant transparent glass pyramid built by I.M. Pei in 1989 sparkles with myriad bright reflections. Although it is partly functional (it serves to illuminate the museum's new underground galleries), this edifice, or more precisely its position in a setting with an obviously very different style, was the subject of much heated debate, not totally dissimilar to that aroused by the construction of the Eiffel Tower a century earlier.

Paris: the Eiffel Tower "Oh Eiffel Tower, thou shepherdess . . . " This is how Guillaume Apollinaire, at the dawn of the 20th century, greeted the modernistic beauty of what was then a very controversial monument. Despite such controversy, the Tower has since become the best-known symbol of Paris. Built at the time of the Universal Exhibition of 1889, it represents the triumph of architecture in metal, combining strength with grace. From the top, nearly a thousand feet above the ground, the view is superb. The apartment blocks overlooking the Seine on the right illustrate a modern aspect of Paris, while at the tip of the Ile aux Cygnes the Statue of Liberty, given to the city by the American community in Paris in 1885, faces west towards its elder sister in New York.

Paris: structures of glass At the end of the 19th century, in a Paris that had become frozen into a neo-classical mould since the time of Haussmann, Hector Guimard (the "Architectural Anarchist") brought *Art Nouveau* to the capital's streets. The entrance to the Porte Dauphine station, on the edge of the Bois de Boulogne, is one of the few survivors of the dozens of Guimard's constructions for the Métro. It is a prime example of the baroque forms that *Art Nouveau* had been evolving for twenty years. A modest Métro entrance, which thousands of Parisians were to use every day, was decorated with a floral design incorporating plants and insects, using a subtle mixture of freestone, iron, cast iron, Auvergne lava, enamel, lacquer and glass. The "dragonfly" motif dear to *Art Nouveau* can be seen in the elegance of the canopy, with its glass "membrane" and delicate metal "veins".

The same principles were applied at the beginning of this century to the large glass dome over the centre of *Printemps*, the department store. Here, eight metal pillars rise six floors, elegantly supporting the glass, through which light filters down all the way to the ground floor. Paper birds, lightly suspended in space, reinforce the sense of harmony thus produced.

Modern Paris Architectural aesthetics underwent a profound change in France after 1945. Whole districts of Paris were transformed, such as Les Halles, and others, such as La Défense, were created from scratch.

The Centre Pompidou, in the heart of Old Paris, has been the home of contemporary art since 1977. The building's avant-garde architecture is striking, almost shocking. An enormous steel frame encloses vast walls of glass. All the functional parts of the building (in particular the ventilation and heating pipes) were deliberately placed on the outside. Painted in simple, bright colours they serve to reinforce the powerful, modernist effect of the whole construction. It is a museum of modern art, but also a cultural centre, with a cinema, lecture theatres, experimental music workshops, and so forth. Every year the Centre receives millions of visitors, and the crowds who gather on the piazza in front of it vividly reflect the cosmopolitan life to be found here.

To the west of the Champs-Elysées, the futuristic geometry of La Défense is another sign of the desire for urban renewal. It is both a residential area and Paris' major commercial district, and is based around a vast pedestrian precinct. Among the spectacular constructions are the Arche, a huge, hollow cube (Notre-Dame could fit inside it), covered in white Carrara marble and Calder's *Stabile Rouge*.

Paris: the Musée d'Orsay Paris' newest museum has been built in the imposing setting of the old railway station of the same name. Opened in 1986, it is entirely devoted to 19th-century art, concentrating on the different forms of artistic expression that were in vogue between 1848 and 1914, from painting to photography and cinema. Works of all kinds, including a large collection of Impressionist and Neo-impressionist paintings, are kept on permanent display. A number of works by sculptors (such as Pradier, Carpaux and Maillol) have also been acquired to fill the museum's cavernous spaces.

Versailles The Château de Versailles was deliberately conceived by Louis XIV as the magnificent symbol of a reign that was both brilliant and absolute. Its majestic façades, including the Midi wing (*above*) overlook the gardens and the 17,000-hectare, landscaped park. All this was built from nothing, driven by the king's overweening desire to impose the royal will on nature itself. This authority was to last a century, until the upheavals of the French Revolution.

Louis XIV's successors were keen to add even further to the splendour of the interiors. The best example of this is undoubtedly the Galerie des Glaces, or Hall of Mirrors.

The gardens of Versailles The gardens of Versailles are Le Nôtre's masterpiece, and Louis XIV himself decided on the protocol for visiting them. Let us stop too, and admire the Pool of Apollo, the work of Tubi. Made from gilded lead from a design by Le Brun, it represents daybreak, with the chariot of Apollo, god of the sun (Louis' own emblem), rising from amongst monsters of the sea to illuminate the earth.

Times and fashions change, and the setting for the Petit Trianon, built by Louis XV for Mme de Pompadour, is a little different. Marie-Antoinette delighted in the "rustic" life here, and this landscaped park, with its charming Temple of Love (*left*) still conjures up the image of courtly entertainment beneath the trees.

Strasbourg and Colmar Alsace, in the east, was for so long the stage where Germany and France tore one another to pieces, but now shows the two countries fully reconciled. Echoes of the past are found in Strasbourg (*opposite*) with its old quarter of "Little France", and Colmar, with its "Little Venice". The old, half-timbered houses are scrupulously well-maintained. Their colourful, decorated façades are reflected in still waters previously used by tanners and market gardeners.

Strasbourg is now the seat of the European Parliament, and the symbol of the new Europe; a Europe built with difficulty, but that seems guided by historical necessity, and one to which the majority of French people are committed.

A land of coal and steel For more than a century and a half the mining industry profoundly influenced the whole of life in the north of France. It made this a region of major economic importance, and coal became the source of energy used for the first industrial revolution, leaving its traces everywhere in the dark countryside of the "Black Country", and punctuating its landscape with pits and slag heaps. Much has changed since those days. The harsh reality of modern economics led to radical and dramatic unemployment, pit closures and redeployments of the workforce in the years between 1970 and 1980.

Giverny At the end of the last century, Claude Monet, one of the greatest French painters, came to live on the border between his native Normandy and the Ile-de-France. Here, at Giverny on the banks of the Epte, he established a magnificent water garden, with the famous pond of water lilies (and its Japanese bridge) that were to be a source of inspiration to him for nearly forty years. The Musée de l'Orangerie, in Paris, which was specially designed for his work, has on permanent display the vast mural panels in which Monet expressed the essence of his art. At Giverny, the "water flower border", as Proust called it, is still there, providing the visitor with a never-ending array of colours and reflections.

Normandy Dotted along the sunken lanes that cut across the countryside of Auge, with its cider-apple trees and peaceful, grazing cattle, family mansions and enormous tracts of farmland testify to the long-established agricultural prosperity of the area. Clay is found in abundance in the region and was used to make the cob for the walls, held in place in its netting by the half-timbering. Scattered around a manor such as this at Caudemer with its large pond, would be an array of outbuildings, housing the mill to pulp the apples, the cider press, the apple store, the cowsheds and the dairy. Normandy is rich and fat, like its own celebrated Camembert and Livarot cheeses, both of which must ideally be eaten when very ripe. There's no wine here, but plenty of good frothy cider, and Calvados, that apple liqueur that is drunk during festive meals, giving guests the "trou Normand" so they regain the appetite they had when they began. The Normans think of everything . . .

Mont Saint-Michel (*preceding pages*) At the mouth of the Couesnon, which divides Normandy from Brittany, and surrounded by treacherous quicksand and racing tides, lies Mont Saint-Michel. In the 10th century, Benedictine monks established a community on this granite islet, gradually building a monastery and cloister, and the abbey church perched on the summit. In the 13th century ramparts were added, turning it into an impregnable fortress. The architecture is full of contrasts. The buildings, such as the towering north buttress known as "the Wonder", even the "Chasm" stairway leading to the monastery, are outwardly majestic and severe, but the interiors have a luminous, intangible grace. There is something magical here, an atmosphere of ever-present legend in this imposing setting, between sea, sky, and sand.

Through a succession of three fortified gates, today's tourists, like the pilgrims of old, enter the main street of the medieval village, with its souvenir sellers and its restaurants. This local trade flourished even in the Middle Ages, when pilgrims made sure they had saints' medallions to ward off the dangers of the quicksand and sudden tides on the route to what was called "Saint-Michel of the perilous sea".

Cap Fréhel Brittany is the westernmost point of France, slicing the ocean like the stem of a ship. All along the Armorican and Finistère coasts are the signs of the age-old confrontation between the rocks, the sea and the wind. In Breton, Ar-Mor means "the country of the sea", while Finistère, from the Latin "Finis terrae", or "Land's End", is self-explanatory. For hundreds of miles all that can be seen are massive blocks of sandstone and granite, torn asunder by the unceasing onslaught of the seas, in an astonishing variety of colours (from dark grey and ochre to pink and reddish). Here on the Emerald Coast, at Cap Fréhel (*left*) red sandstone cliffs plunge vertically into the turquoise waves. The cries of gulls and cormorants fill the air, and when it is foggy, mingle with the foghorn's penetrating note. The beam of the lighthouse on the clifftop can be seen 75 miles out to sea. Every hour of every day, somewhere out there is a Breton sailor.

Etretat Much further north, in Upper Normandy, the plateau forming the countryside of Caux faces the sea in the majestic cliffs of the Alabaster Coast, which are, without question, most impressive around Etretat. Under a light, misty sky, lies a long beach of pebbles forever washed by the foaming surf. It is flanked by two high, white cliffs of chalk, the Upper Cliff with its small sailors' chapel consecrated to Notre-Dame de la Garde, and the Lower Cliff, with its towering rocky arch (la Porte d'Aval or Lower Gate) and its mysterious Pinnacle.

Dinan Sheltering upstream from the estuaries of the Breton rivers, a number of small port towns that once thrived on trade and now thrive on yachting, still retain their heritage within surrounding granite walls. Dinan, on the banks of the Rance, is one such town; its port nestles in a steep valley now spanned by a great viaduct. Surrounded by defences built in the 13th and 14th centuries its narrow streets wind down the steep bank from the plateau overlooking the river. These streets have names echoing the crafts and mercantile activities of the past, and are full of bustle and activity throughout the summer tourist season.

The Norman countryside The bocage, a lightly-wooded countryside, is typical of the Armorican Massif. But it also occurs farther afield, particularly towards the east, in Normandy and the Auge. The waters of hundreds of small rivers and streams wind through rolling hills covered in oak trees, elms and beeches, and flow across green pastures criss-crossed by quickset hedges and orchards.

The Breton Coast At the Pointe
d'Amorique, off Brest, as well as
farther south in the Morbihan Bay,
with its hundreds of small rocky
islands, the charm of the Breton
coasts and their latticework of granite
is irresistible. The Atlantic winds and
the ocean waves have carved these
coasts with a strange combination of
ferocity and gentleness.

Douarnenez, deep within the great
bay of the same name, south of the
Armorican peninsula, has always
been a major fishing port for
sardines, tuna and mackerel, and also
lobsters, which the fishing vessels
catch far to the south, off the
Mauritanian coast.

Carnac Mystery surrounds Carnac and its lines of standing stones. Over an area nearly three miles across there are close to 3000 of these granite megaliths, divided into three groups. The largest of these, the Menec alignments, has 1099 menhirs (the highest 12 feet tall), arranged in 11 parallel lines.

The stones were erected in Neolithic times and at the beginning of the Bronze Age, and they are probably religious monuments associated with the cult of the dead. The directions of the alignments, however, correspond to the positions of sunrise at the summer solstice or the equinoxes, so they may be evidence of sun-worship.

Whatever the explanation, menhirs and dolmens (chambered tombs) are an inseparable part of the Breton countryside, evoking the Celtic past, with its druids, fairies and magic spells. This enormous dolmen (several of the stones are more than 18 feet long) opens onto the 982 menhirs in the rows at Kermario.

The Loire Valley: Chambord
(*following pages*) A flawless marriage of time and space, the Château de Chambord, with its 365 chimneys, reveals the perfect balance, elegance, and majesty of its architecture reflected in its lake. The French Renaissance, still dazzled by its discovery of Italian forms, reached its height here in the Loire Valley.

François I asked Leonardo da Vinci to draw up a plan for a palace worthy of him. When the king died in 1547 most of the castle had already been built, but the building was finished by Louis XIV a century later. In the soft light of the Loire Valley, Chambord radiates the splendour and grace of its many works of art, such as its sweeping staircases, its sculptures, and its magnificent rooms with elegant wood panellings, tapestries and other decorations.

François I initially came to Chambord to indulge his passion for hunting. Hunting parties are still regularly organized in the great park. This is surrounded by a wall twenty miles long and has been a hunting reserve since 1948.

The Château de Chenonceau
(*preceding pages*) The Château de
Chenonceau is less regal than
Chambord, but more picturesque. It
extends right across the river Cher. It
was built at the beginning of the 16th
century by the wife of a tax collector
and at that time consisted only of the
main rectangular building. Diane de
Poitiers, mistress of Henri II, and then
Catherine de Médici, his wife, turned
it into the superb building it is today.
Catherine constructed the two-storey
gallery above the bridge that had been
built by her beautiful rival. That
rivalry is also reflected in the two
gardens that face each other across
the entrance terrace on the banks of
the river. Until the assassination of
Henri III, incredibly lavish fêtes were
held here. What strikes us today is the
harmony of its bucolic setting, where
the waters, the wide banks of the
gardens, and the foliage of the park
all enhance the elegance of the
buildings.

Saint-Aignan An old stone bridge, a
river, and a small village with houses
scattered over a peaceful hillside are
overlooked by a Romanesque
collegiate church and a Renaissance
château, itself built on the ruins of
fortifications dating from feudal
times. This is Saint-Aignan on the
banks of the Cher, in the heart of a
region of forests and vineyards. But it
could be any one of the hundreds of
similar villages that present their
smiling faces over the serene, almost
timeless hills and valleys of "France's
heartland".

Massif Central: the volcanoes of Auvergne The volcanic region of the Auvergne stretches more than 60 miles from the north to the south of the Massif Central. It is a sight of constant wonder, and one that is unique in France: enormous masses of rock in jagged escarpments, deep valleys, and steep-sided lakes of crystal-clear water. All this was produced by intense volcanic activity at the end of the Tertiary, and by the glaciation that followed. In the Dore mountains, to the south of Clermont-Ferrand, the capital of the Auvergne,

the Massif de Sancy sums up the region's character. Its contorted hills have a wild and rugged, brooding beauty. From the summits, on a very clear day one can see as far as the Alps of Dauphiné.

To the west of Clermont-Ferrand runs the long chain of the Puys, 112 extinct volcanoes otherwise known as the Monts de Dôme, stretching twenty miles. Their scenery of cones and craters bring more than just a hint of a lunar landscape. The Puy de Côme *(opposite)* has two craters, one inside the other.

Le Puy-en-Velay In a deep gorge cut by the Loire, still close to its source, Le-Puy-en-Velay lies in a stunning setting of hills formed of volcanic rocks that are resistant to erosion. Two enormous, monolithic blocks rise in its centre: the Aiguilhe rock (magnificently crowned by the chapel of Saint-Michel), and the Corneille rock. For more than a century, the latter has borne a gigantic statue of the Virgin Mary and Child, a reminder that for centuries the town and the basilica near the rock were one of the most famous sites of pilgrimage in Christian Europe. Even the kings of France prayed at the shrine.

Lavoûte-Chilhac To the north-east of Le Puy is Lavoûte-Chilhac (*right*), with its strange double row of houses lining the inside of a sharp bend in the river Allier. At the head of the narrow neck of land, a Gothic church lies within a Benedictine monastery whose semicircular ground-plan seems to follow the bend of the river.

Château-Rocher The history of the Auvergne is almost as turbulent as its volcanic past. It was the centre of Gaulish resistance to the Roman invasion, and in the Middle Ages castles were sited all over the region. There was scarcely a jagged peak that was not crowned with one of these powerful fortresses (like the Château-Rocher among the gorges of La Sioule). Their sombre isolation fires the imagination to this day.

But the region is also famous for works of a different nature: the intricate works of art produced by the patient lacemakers of Le Puy.

Dordogne: Collonges la Rouge

Collonges la Rouge lies to the west of the Massif Central facing the Brive basin, where the hilly countryside has already taken on something of the character of the South. Buildings in Collonges are made from warm red sandstone, whose colour, shading to ochre glows from every wall. The village was founded in the 8th century, and subsequently developed around the fortified church and the priory. In the 16th century it was a place where high-ranking officials came to spend time in the country, and small country seats, manor houses and buildings adorned with towers arose everywhere. Signs of this can be seen in the robust but elegant architecture of this simple farm.

Rural life here continues to revolve around the livestock markets, traditional occasions that, despite modernization and changes in agricultural practices, show no sign of losing their popular appeal.

Truffles and foie gras On the rocky "causses" (limestone plateaux) of Périgord, with their woods of stunted oak, or farther south in the dark forests of ilexes of Périgord Noir, grows that culinary prize, the truffle. A black, scented mushroom, it grows some nine inches underground on the roots of oak trees, and is found by using the keen sense of smell of a dog or a sow. When the animal starts to dig it up, all the "caveux" – as a truffle-hunter is called – has to do is to move the animal away and carefully extract the mushroom using a hooked stick.

Every year, thousands of geese and ducks are raised in the farmyards of Périgord and Quercy for the production of one of the specialities of the region: foie gras. Foie gras, which is made by force-feeding the birds over several months, culminating in a three-week intensive phase, should be eaten with Montbazillac, a syrupy white wine from the Bergerac region, or a great white Bordeaux such as Sauternes, served chilled.

Les Eyzies From the earliest times (as long ago as 150,000 BC), the valleys of Périgord and their overhanging rocks offered particularly favourable living sites for prehistoric man. The valley of the Vézère is especially rich in prehistoric remains. Near the famous site of Cro-Magnon, are dwellings at Les Eyzies that were carved from the base of the massive limestone walls that hem in the Vézère, which then flowed some thirty yards above its present level. For several tens of thousands of years men and women lived in these shelters, leaving many traces of their activities, such as ash from fires, tools, and weapons.

Lascaux Not far upstream, the cave at Lascaux has a superb collection of 1500 drawings and paintings from the Magdalenian period (17,000 BC), forming a unique record of wall and prehistoric painting. On the walls of the four galleries, coloured silhouettes of cattle, horses, deer, bison and mammoths are drawn with an amazing surety of line and an overwhelming sense of movement. Because of the risk of serious deterioration of these works of art, following their sudden exposure to the air after thousands of years in sealed conditions, the cave was closed in 1963. Since 1983, an identical replica has been open to the public.

La Roque Gageac (*following pages*) As it crosses the Périgord plateau the Dordogne follows sweeping curves, and downstream of Sarlat it flows at the base of steep rocks topped by castles obviously built in more turbulent times. Between the walled town of Domme (upstream) and the fortresses of Castelnaud and Beynac, whose protective outlines loom on cliffs overhanging the river, the whole of La Roque Gageac is built at the foot of its "Golden Cliff" crowned with ilexes. Under the jutting rocks, lies the tiny village with roofs of stone, and the two steeply gabled buildings of the Manoir de Tarde, with its tower and mullioned windows.

Countryside near Salignac The austere beauty of the grey and golden rocks of the limestone plateau of Périgord Noir can be seen in the steep escarpment of Martel (on the south-western side of the Massif Central), where the woods of oak and black pine are broken by the harsh solitude of rocky coombes covered in dry summer grasses. Farther west, towards Salignac and Sarlat, large expanses of meadows and ploughed fields, growing cereals and tobacco, lap rounded hills (called "pechs") covered in ilexes. It is a land of sharp contrasts, where rich, fertile lowlands adjoin the dry, rocky uplands.

The Poitou Marshes The Poitou Marshes form a strange countryside to the west of Niort, where they straddle the River Sèvre, and extend almost as far as the ocean. The most attractive part has been given the delightful name of "Green Venice". Poplars and willows stand on the edge of a labyrinth of waterways (known as "conches" and "rigoles") enclosing pastures and fruit-growing orchards. Their foliage filters the summer sun, casting sombre reflections on the silent water. Low, whitewashed houses clustered in villages on islands in the marshes are home to the "maraîchins". They breed dairy cows, but also spend a lot of time fishing for eels and hunting snipe. In this part of the world, people move around on black punts pushed with "shovels", and in the most remote parts of the marshlands, harvest and livestock are still transported in this way.

Cognac Since the 17th century, the home of Charentes liqueur brandy has been at Cognac. Here, in the chalky furrows of the valley, people cultivate the white grape from which the famous brandy is made.

The wine is heated over a low, naked flame in a beaten copper still. The first distillation produces an impure spirit known as "brouillis". The second, known simply as "la bonne" ("the right one"), gives, once the unwanted substances have been removed, what is known as the "eau-de-vie de coeur". This is then stored in oak vats for an average of between five and forty years. In the storehouses of Cognac the "Fine Champagne" (named after the Grande and Petite Champagne, that is the area immediately around the town) acquires its beautiful amber colour, which it retains while stored in casks made from Limousin oak or in wicker-covered glass demijohns.

Les Landes South of Bordeaux, on the road to Spain, the countryside changes completely. The vast marshy plain of Les Landes extends from the Gironde to the Adour. During the last century this was transformed into a vast forest of maritime pines in an attempt to check the advance of the great sand dunes of the Atlantic coast. It is a light and airy forest, permeated by the smell of resin.

The T.G.V. The High Speed Train (T.G.V.) is surely one of the most spectacular successes of modern French industry. The latest example of this advanced technology is the T.G.V.-Atlantique (covering the Paris-Nantes route). Here it is seen setting its first world speed record, travelling at 300 miles per hour. A few days later this record was itself broken, when it set a new one of 312 miles per hour.

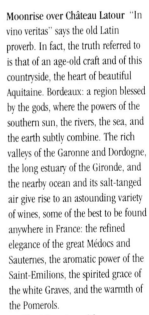

Moonrise over Château Latour "In vino veritas" says the old Latin proverb. In fact, the truth referred to is that of an age-old craft and of this countryside, the heart of beautiful Aquitaine. Bordeaux: a region blessed by the gods, where the powers of the southern sun, the rivers, the sea, and the earth subtly combine. The rich valleys of the Garonne and Dordogne, the long estuary of the Gironde, and the nearby ocean and its salt-tanged air give rise to an astounding variety of wines, some of the best to be found anywhere in France: the refined elegance of the great Médocs and Sauternes, the aromatic power of the Saint-Emilions, the spirited grace of the white Graves, and the warmth of the Pomerols.

After it has ripened for many months in the sun, the wine matures in the dark, cool wine stores (here, that of Château Lafite). Bordeaux wines, especially the reds, can stand the test of time. To quote a contemporary son of Bordeaux, the writer Philippe Sollers, "In veritate, vinum".

Bordeaux On the edge of the quays built along the Garonne, the Place de la Bourse and the magnificent set of buildings that enclose it are perfect illustrations of the commercial and financial boom that Bordeaux underwent in the 18th century. The Grand Theatre, the Allées de Tourny and what used to be the Place Dauphine (now Place Gambetta) all date from this time, and help to make this one of the most beautiful cities in France. On the far side of the "Port de la lune", where cargoes of claret used to be despatched to England, a huge harbour complex now extends. The industrial and petrochemical ports of Bassens, Ambès and Verdon now stretch from here down to the head of the Gironde estuary.

Saint-Jean-Pied-de-Port In Lower Navarre, in the Basque country, Saint-Jean-Pied-de-Port was the last staging post for pilgrims on the route to Santiago de Compostela before they crossed the Pyrénées through the Port de Roncevaux (the pass in the mountains where valiant Roland perished many years ago). Beneath what was once the citadel, the old bridge remains, as do the white houses with flower-decked balconies overlooking the Nive. Having crossed the river, the road ahead leads to Spain, taking us to other scenes and memories of other times.

The Valley of the Aspe In the high valleys of Béarn, as here in the bleak Aspe Valley, the traditional pastoral life still thrives. From May to July, the flocks gradually climb to the high mountain meadows that they will leave in October. Some will even go as far as the heathlands to the north of Pau, in accordance with the customs and rights that the mountain-dwellers have preserved intact from medieval times. The sheep's-milk cheeses of the Pyrénées are well-known, but ewe's milk is also used to make Roquefort. The Aspe Valley is part of the Pyrénées National Park, and it is one of the few places where brown bears still manage precariously to survive.

Lourdes Inspired by the extraordinary religious fervour of a little fourteen-year-old shepherdess, Bernadette Soubirous, the fame of Lourdes and its pilgrimages rapidly became accepted. Since the end of the last century, every year during the summer, invalids, pilgrims and visitors have come in their hundreds of thousands to this little town on the banks of the Pau. Heart-rending scenes take place on the vast Square of the Rosary outside the basilica, where invalids come driven by the fierce desire for a cure to their suffering. Even ignoring the controversies that such things inevitably generate, the phenomenon bears witness to a popular faith of a kind found very rarely in this day and age.

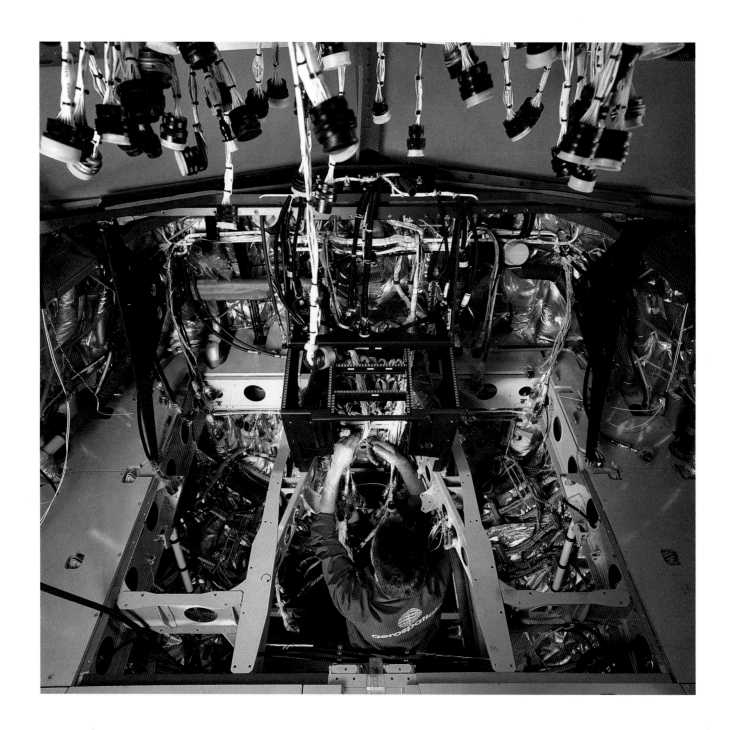

Toulouse Toulouse was the base for the famous Aéropostale company and for the airlines that maintained the links with the French colonial empire and South America. Following this tradition, the town has become one of the great European centres of aircraft construction. Here, in the vast hangars of the Aérospatiale company, Airbus 320's are assembled and cockpits wired and fitted out. This aircraft, and others in the series, are built by a joint consortium of French, British, German and Belgian firms.

Albi On the banks of the river Tarn that has grown placid after leaving the last foothills of the south-western Massif Central, lies Albi "le rouge", with its 11th-century bridge, its narrow, twisting streets and houses of interlocking bricks. Overlooking the town is the cathedral of Sainte-Cécile and the fortress-like episcopal palace, symbols of the Church's victory over the Cathar heresy.

Sainte-Cécile The great cathedral was built at the end of the 13th century in the southern Gothic style and the finishing touches were gradually added. The 15th-century chancel is in the late flamboyant style, and is divided by a superb, ornate rood-screen. Before the Revolution it was adorned with 96 statues, but only a few remain: Christ on the Cross, the Virgin and Saint John, above Adam and Eve. Dazzling paintings by Italian artists decorate the walls and vault of the nave.

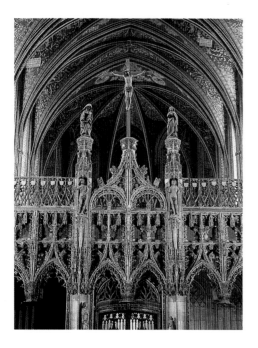

The "Chaos" of Montpellier
(*following pages*) On the great limestone plateau, south of the Massif Central, strange stone landscapes, sculptured by erosion, appear. Their sheer size and the way their strata, ledges and vertical walls were formed make them look like vast, ruined towns. Extending over 120 hectares of the Causse Noir, for example, is the "Chaos", an extraordinary rocky formation called "Old Montpellier" by the local shepherds. Until the end of the last century it was hidden by an impenetrable forest inhabited by ferocious wolves, and believed to be a town that had been cursed and which was haunted by the Devil. These rocks are a strange sight; when seen by the changing light at dawn and dusk the effect is quite eerie.

Elne About five miles south of Perpignan, lies Elne. Here, adjoining the cathedral of Sainte-Eulalie, the cloister (*left*) offers cool shade against the searing heat of the summer. The capitals of its columns are magnificently sculpted, and it is one of the finest examples of high Romanesque art in the region.

Collioure At the foot of the eastern Pyrénées in sunny Roussillon, villages that still bear witness of their ancient role as tiny centres of shipping nestle in the rocky bays and coves of the Côte Vermeille. This is Collioure, dominated by the Albères and their sun-scorched terraces where the black vine of Roussillon, the "grenache", is grown. Immortalized by famous painters (including Braque, Matisse and Picasso), the port and the vivid colours of its flower-bedecked houses stand out against the blue backdrop of the sky and the Mediterranean, where, at nightfall, the men will catch bluefish by lamplight.

Nîmes The towns of Nîmes, Orange and Arles all bear witness to the brilliance of the Gallo-Roman civilization that influenced the history of Provence so profoundly. A number of impressive monuments still survive.

The amphitheatre of the Arena at Nîmes is the finest remaining in what was once the Roman world and was the scene of many gladiatorial contests. It is probably no coincidence if, under the influence of the other great culture of south-western Europe, that of Spain, great bull-fights are now held here every year. The season reaches a climax with a "Féria" which embraces the whole town, day and night.

The Camargue (*preceding pages*)
To the south of Arles the vast marshy plain of the Camargue extends into the Rhône Delta. Although the area of cultivated land has been significantly increased over the past fifty years, the large, wild, southern part is a nature reserve. Here, amongst pools and lagoons directly linked to the sea, beneath the vast canopy of the Mediterranean sky, a great variety of wild animals roam at will. It is a place for birds, such as the vivid pink flamingoes that live in vast colonies. But there are also herds (or "manades") of wild bulls, which will be used in the "cockade races" that take place in Provence (particularly in Arles and Nîmes). Their herdsmen (often in completely authentic regional costume) are superb horsemen, and just as in the past, ride "Camargue" horses; some claim the breed has persisted here since prehistoric times.

Orange The ancient theatre of Orange, which is equally well-preserved, was built in the reign of Augustus (whose statue we see here). Today it is the scene of one of the many artistic festivals that have become something of a feature of modern Provence. In the one here, Les Chorégies, some of the best voices of contemporary opera are able to take advantage of the exceptional acoustics that the Romans achieved in this theatre.

Avignon The famous "Pont d'Avignon" of the song was over half a mile in length, its twenty-two arches spanning the two branches of the River Rhône. It was partly destroyed when the Rhône flooded in the 17th century. In the background, the Palace of the Popes reminds us of the town's glorious past: in the 14th century it became the (disputed) capital of the Christian world. From the outside, the palace looks like a fortress, in striking contrast to the interior, which shows typical Italian refinement in the decoration and architecture, particularly in the frescoes, which were the work of some of the greatest painters of the Trecento. High culture is found, these days, in the Festival of Dramatic Art, which was created by J. Vilar in 1947, and which every year attracts actors and spectators from all over Europe to the old town.

The colours of Provence Beneath a brilliant sky, the vibrant colours in this landscape are matched by the ceaseless, shrill cry of the cicadas. The dark purple expanse enhanced by brilliant greens and yellows gives this Provençal lavender field the feel of a Van Gogh painting.

Les Baux-de-Provence Like an impregnable eyrie, this fortified town (*left*) still seems to dominate the surrounding area. The turbulent history of this part of the world is reflected in its wild grandeur. But with its ruined castle impudently built on the cliffs of the ravines, the town and religious buildings that overlook streets, some of which were carved from solid rock, this is not just picturesque. Rather, it is an assertion of a pride as old as the hills.

In the narrow streets of the part of the town that is still inhabited, the old houses bear witness to its former splendour. In those days, the lords of Baux, who had links with the most powerful families in Europe, boasted that their lineage could be traced back to Balthazar, one of the three kings present at Christ's nativity. Each year at Christmas, at midnight mass, the shepherds come to the church of Saint-Vincent to make an offering of a new-born lamb . . .

Marseille The glamour of the Old Port, the shady streets that run down to the quays or the Canebière, those strange (and rare) moments of silence and solitude in a world that is normally filled with noise, with cries, with colours, and with the ceaseless bustle of a horde of people from everywhere under the sun, speaking every imaginable tongue . . . all this is Marseille, the second city of France and its premier port. A gateway to the Orient and open to both its exotic splendours and misfortunes, Marseille has always been a turbulent, yet cheerful and utterly cosmopolitan place. Strangely, despite being one of the oldest cities in Western Europe (it was originally a Greek colony founded by Phoceans from Asia Minor well before the Roman conquest), it has preserved few marks of its long history. It is as if the city has always been indifferent to its past, and bound up in an eternal present, as intemperate as the Mistral or sudden love. It is easy to be infatuated with Marseille, despite everything, just as it is.

Monaco In the far south-east of France, set on a narrow rocky slope plunging down to the Mediterranean, the minute Principality of Monaco displays its wealth and splendour in the way it has grown vertically. The dearth of available ground space has been compensated by the construction of skyscrapers, the use of basements (as for the huge aquarium of the Oceanographic Museum) and the systematic reclamation of land from the sea. With the advantage of a location that enjoys both constant sunshine and a non-existent taxation system (it is difficult to say which aspect makes it more heavenly), the Monagasques have succeeded in turning their town into a mecca for gambling and luxury tourism. The royal family obligingly plays its part in a larger-than-life world, where marriages and society scandals provide the touch of the exotic that the average French person likes to read about in the headlines.

Monte-Carlo Monaco's legend was
mainly built on gambling, and to the
whole world it is summed up in one
name, Monte-Carlo. The Casino,
luxury hotels, sumptuous villas, and
gardens full of flowers provide what
has come to be regarded as the
essential setting for the dramas and
miracles dictated nightly by the
whims of the roulette wheel. Some
prefer the daytime beauty, a short
distance away towards La Napoule, of
the coast at Esterel; a wild,
untouched, coastal landscape that
quite obviously merits that evocative
name, the Côte d'Azur.

Corsica Some 100 miles out to sea from Nice, the "Island of Beauty" is cloaked in a finery of natural colours and scents. It is a land of mountainous slopes covered in maquis, of high and narrow valleys, and rocky coasts plunging down into a clear blue sea. It is a secret island too, with a brooding pride, divided (or even torn) between its loyalty to a union with France that dates back many years, and its demands for an independence that also draws on a very ancient tradition.

Bonifacio, at the extreme southern point of the island, is an old medieval town, whose fortifications and houses rise above the long channel leading to the port.

The Alps: La Vanoise National Park In the heart of Savoie, the La Vanoise National Park covers 53,000 hectares of the massif of the same name, rising to 12,000 feet at the summit of the Grande Casse. Ibex and chamois, threatened with extinction thirty years ago, now breed in peace and their numbers are constantly increasing. The flora is particularly varied with over one thousand species of flowers. In the photograph (*above*), with the Grande Casse rising in the background, is the dark red dotted pink of martagon lilies, the velvety blue of gentians, and even the golden yellow of sulphur anemones.

The Tignes Dam Since the end of the last century, great use has been made of "white coal" and the hydroelectric power that it provides. Many dams have been built in the Alps, such as this one at Tignes, which entered service in 1953, when much reconstruction and modernization was undertaken after World War II. Built with great difficulty – mainly because of the harsh climate – on a tributary of the Isère, it took three years to finish and is 540 feet high, including 60 feet of foundations. The old village of Tignes (re-built higher up) lies beneath the reservoir, which supplies several major power stations.

Chamonix Farther north, at the foot of Mont Blanc (which rises over 12,000 feet above sea-level), Chamonix is the international centre for mountaineering. It is possible to go there simply as a tourist, of course, taking the rack railway up the mountain as far as the Mer de Glace, or in the cable-car as high up as the Aiguille du Midi (*opposite*). But Chamonix is also the home to that famous fraternity, the mountain guides, who undertake the major climbs, and whose exploits, since the original conquest of Mont Blanc in 1786, have continually added to alpine legend.

Courchevel Lying between the Tarentaise and the Maurienne, La Vanoise Massif has both vast snowy slopes and plentiful sunshine. Winter sports centres have proliferated here in recent years, particularly in the "Trois Vallées". At Courchevel there are four, at altitudes between 1300 and 1850 metres (*below*) on the slope of the Doron de Bozel, and all equipped with ultra-modern ski-lifts. Tourism in summer is also becoming more popular: in the keen alpine air the views of neighbouring summits are magnificent.

La Grande Chartreuse Deep in the heart of one of the five great rocky massifs of the Pre-Alps, lies the monastery of La Grande Chartreuse, imposing its own silence on the "desert" where Saint Bruno founded it ten centuries ago. Its superb setting, among the solitude of the forests that fringe high limestone escarpments, is conducive to contemplation and meditation. The monastery, whose buildings date from the 17th century, is a place of peace and prayer and is therefore, quite rightly, closed to visitors. Any interested tourist can find information about the life of the order – which has seventeen other monasteries throughout the world – in the Carthusian museum of La Correrie, lower down the mountain.

Lyon Lyon is at the confluence of the Rhône and the Saône, at the northern end of the great European crossroads formed by the Rhône Valley. For twenty centuries this town has been a great metropolis and, during this time, many monuments have been erected on the banks of both rivers and on its hills. On the hill of Fourvière stands Saint-Jean cathedral (*opposite*), while that of La Croix-Rousse has a labyrinth of "traboules" (narrow streets) that thread their way through the tall houses where thirty thousand "canuts" (silk workers) used to work. For several centuries Lyon was the weaving capital of France, particularly for silk. Nowadays, as its population nears the million mark, it has become a great industrial and commercial city, and is the centre of one of the most dynamic regions of modern France. It is also a city where people have a gift for the good things in life (the cuisine of Lyon has acquired a justly merited reputation for excellence), and it is far enough from Paris to have been able to develop its own identity and a cultural independence that is now beginning to assume European dimensions.

The Rhône Valley All along the
Rhône Valley from Lyon to Avignon,
vineyards and orchards reap the
benefits of an extremely favourable
climate. Among the wines from these
Côtes du Rhône, the finest are those
from the "Côte Rôtie" (seen here)
that derive their colour and alcohol
from the baking sun. Even in Roman
times these wines were sought by
connoisseurs. On the left bank of the
Rhône around Vienne and Valence,
and farther south near Carpentras, a
vast amount of fruit is cultivated
(peaches, pears, cherries, melons,
apricots and strawberries), and the
whole region is really one big
orchard. In spring, the blossom of the
trees powders the Rhône with pink
and white throughout its long descent
towards the Mediterranean.

The Jura The mountains and valleys of the Jura range, on the eastern borders of France, are clad in magnificent forests. Among these vast, rocky expanses, which are covered with beech, pine, sessile oak, birch and hornbeam, the precious freedom of the wide outdoors, tinged with adventure, can be found in long rambles in the woods.

Meursault and Beaune Hillside vineyards extend for forty miles south of Dijon, the capital of fertile Burgundy. Their names are unforgettable to all lovers of wine and the words themselves give a hint of their magic. . . . There is, the Côte de Nuits, around Nuits-Saint-George – Chambertin, Clos-Vougeot, Romanée-Conti – all particularly full-bodied red wines that only reach full maturity after eight or ten years. Farther south the Côte de Beaune also produces some great reds with delicate bouquets (Volnay and Pommard, for example). Then there are whites with incomparable flavours, such as Meursault (*opposite*), which is rare in being both dry and mellow.

In contrast to the Bordeaux wines (their eternal rivals!) with their great demesnes and aristocratic overtones, wine production is still by individual growers, linked to particular villages and cooperatives in most of Burgundy.

In the heart of this region, Beaune and its general hospital (*above*), with its multi-coloured, glazed-tile roofs and its finely worked lead finials, is a reminder of the glorious past, when the Grand Duchy of Burgundy extended as far as Flanders. Every year, on the third Sunday in November, the famous sale of the wines from the Hospices de Beaune takes place. This is one of the "Glorious Three" days – with Saturday in Le Clos de Vougeot and Monday in Meursault – devoted to the celebration of the wines from the aptly named Côte d'Or. Having amply sampled the excellence of Burgundy cuisine, all that remains is to get together and sing "Happy sons of Burgundy . . .".

Wines and mushrooms Although perhaps less well-known, the vineyards of the Côte Chalonnaise, like those of Mercurey or Givry, or the Château de Rully (shown here), are still part of the noble area of the Côte d'Or. They form its southernmost point, but the journey does not stop here: on the other side of the little River Grosne, we come to the Mâconnais, then to the Beaujolais (with its vintages now famous as far afield as Japan), Juliénas, Moulin-à-vent, Morgon, Brouilly, and so on.

Much farther north, on the way to Paris, the region of Pouilly-sur-Loire is also known for its white wines and chasselas grapes. Mushrooms are gathered in the woods here; the humid climate causes them to grow in vast numbers. The ones shown here are "elm's ears". The word "ear" is often incorporated into the popular name for mushrooms, such as "asses' ear", "bear's ear", and "thistle ear", while the "holly ear" is another name for chanterelle, which goes so well with a "baveuse" (runny) omelette.

Vézelay On the borders of Morvan and the Paris Basin, the Basilica of Sainte-Madeleine lies behind its ancient defences atop a hill overlooking the wooded valley of the River Cure. It is probably the most beautiful example of Romanesque art in Burgundy. Saint Bernard came here to preach for the Second Crusade; during the Third, Philippe Auguste and Richard the Lionheart arranged to set off together from here for the East. Three portals lead from the huge narthex into the long nave and chancel. The nave is bathed in light; seen here at midsummer, when the pools of light falling on the flagstones from apertures high in the southern wall form a luminous chain, linking the altar cross to the figure of Christ in his glory, carved on the tympanum of the central portal.

Chartres The cathedral of Chartres dominates the plain of La Beauce, for a long time Paris' bread-basket, and its two, 12th-century towers, the "old" and the "new", soar into the sky. The cathedral is the oldest masterpiece of Gothic architecture in France and devoted to the worship of the Virgin Mary, a belief symbolized to this day by pilgrims who come here on foot from Paris. The statuary is extraordinarily varied, but the cathedral's greatest wonder is its beautiful stained-glass windows, which have remained miraculously intact. Some 5000 characters from the Bible or the Lives of the Saints are depicted in medallions against a background of the famous "Chartres blue".

Rheims Rheims is not only, with Epernay, the capital of Champagne. One of the most beautiful Gothic cathedrals, ranking alongside those of Paris, Soissons, Chartres, and Amiens, also stands in its centre. What is particularly striking about Rheims cathedral is the incredibly rich statuary, consisting of 2300 figures, that adorns the exterior. The kings' gallery, above the great rose-window, has 56 statues each more than twelve feet high, reminding us that from the time of Clovis in the 5th century, the coronation of the kings of France took place in Rheims. Among the many religious figures represented in this "stone Bible", which was praised in their day by both Victor Hugo and Ruskin, there is the smiling angel, who seems to be trying to soothe his neighbour, Saint Nicaise, the town's first martyr at the beginning of the 5th century, and to convince him of the prospect of eternal bliss.

Index

Acknowledgements

The publishers would like to thank the following organizations and individuals for their kind permission to reproduce the photographs in this book.
Action Plus 22. **Aérospatiale** 66 left, 66 right. **Campagne Campagne** 28, 32-33, 34, 43, 45, 50-51, 52, 62, 68, 69, 74, 76, 115, 118 bottom left, 125, 128, 129. **J. Allan Cash** 16, 118, 124. **Cephas** 52 left, 78, 88, 90-91, 130-131, 134, 135, 136-137. **Bruce Coleman Ltd** 108-109. **Colorific** 23, 30-31. **Père Hughes Delautre** 139. **Lawrence Delderfield** 120-121. **Explorer** 19, 26, 37 top, 38, 42, 46, 54, 70, 72, 79, 82-83, 84, 87, 91, 94-95, 96-97, 98, 102, 110-111, 113, 122, 123, 126, 127, 140, 142. **Susan Griggs Agency** 15. **Sonia Halliday Photographs** 141. **Robert Harding Library** 6, 14, 24-25, 27, 29, 35, 36, 37 bottom, 110, 117. **Michael Holford** 40. **Denis Hughes-Gilbey Collection** 17, 20, 50, 80-81, 85, 86, 143. **Images** 10-11, 52-53, 60, 61, 64-65, 71. **Landscape Only** 1, 30, 44, 48-49, 56, 58, 59, 62-63, 66-67, 73, 102-103, 104-105, 106, 107, 112-113, 114, 132-133. **Magnum Photos Ltd** 2, 4-5, 8-9, 12-13, 18, 21, 47, 55, 57, 75, 76-77, 116. **S.N.C.F.** 89. **Agence Photographique TOP** 92, 93. **Viewfinder** 41. **M. François Walch** 138.